PROJECT FASHION
FASHION ILLUSTRATION

DRAWING TECHNIQUES

CW01025296

Mila Markle

Eph. 2:8
For it is by grace you have been saved, through faith—
and this is not from yourselves, it is the gift of God

ISBN: 978-1-7764490-5-7 (Paperback)

This book was created without the use of any Artificial Intelligence (AI) or Augmentation. Please support human authors and artists.

First printing edition 2023.

Front cover image and book Illustrations by Mila Markle.
Mila Markle Fashion Books
The Mila Markle logo is a Trademark of Mila Markle Fashion Books.

Table of Contents:

Introduction:

The history of fashion dates as far back as the Mesopotamian period (3000 B.C.E.) This can be seen on ancient discovered art forms, sculptures and pottery. During these ancient times, fashion was used to represent wealth and status. In the 21st Century, fashion is a complex machine driven by psychological, sociological, cultural and commercial forces. With fashion, there is a perpetuating cycle of fashion leaders rebelling against current styles to stand out. The masses are then adopting these trends, which leads to the fashion leaders having to reinvent themselves once more. Fashion designers try to predict what fashion leaders will wear next so that they can adopt the latest trends and styles.

The fashion illustration represent the illustrated version of the designer's idea of the garment before it is constructed. The garment needs to be coloured and rendered to represent the desired fabric convincingly. The fashion illustration will make the design come to life and help the client to visualize what the final product should look like. This includes the choice of colour and fabric as well as what the silhouette will be. Fashion illustrators use various different traditional media such as ink, watercolour, markers etc. to create their art. Digital media is a very popular and convenient option as well.

This book aims to equip the novice fashion designer with basic techniques to create fashion illustrations in their own style. Additionally, you will be guided through the fashion design process which generally consists of: rough drawings, technical drawing and lastly, the fashion illustration. The emphasis will be on learning the basic fashion illustration techniques to add depth to your art and to create different textures. You will also be introduced to the common types of media to choose from to create your line drawings and colour your illustration.

For the novice fashion designer, drawing the croquis can be seen as the first step in creating fashion. This is because it serves as a template for capturing your ideas onto paper before they can be constructed.

The word croquis originates from French meaning "sketch". It refers to the rough drawing of a live model. In the fashion industry, it's the quick drawing of a fashion figure. Differentiation should be made between the croquis used for roughs and the croquis used for fashion illustration.

For the purpose of this book, the term croquis template refers to the symmetrical figure template (with front and back view), which can be used for roughs. When reference is made to fashion figure templates, it refers to templates with dynamic poses intended for the fashion illustration. When they have a dotted vertical line and horizontal lines, they can be used to draw the technical drawing/technical flat. You will find croquis templates at the back of this book, which will serve as a blank canvas for sketching your roughs over without any hassle. ▼

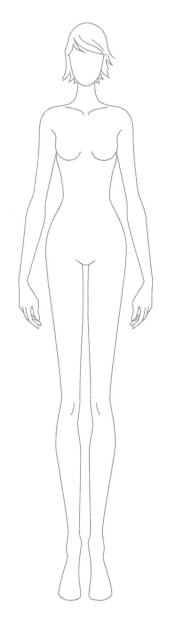 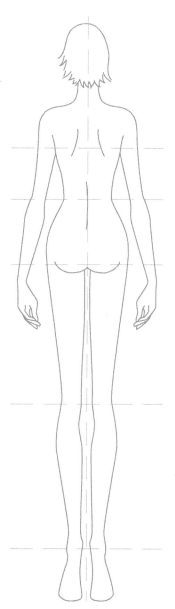

Chapter 1: Drawing Materials

When it comes to fashion illustration, you will see that your choice of drawing materials will influence your fashion drawings. It is good to have a basic knowledge of various types of drawing material to know what is possible to achieve.

Starting off with good quality materials will be of benefit to your artwork. In this book, we will discuss some art materials you should consider using.

"Your attitude is like a box of crayons that colour your world."
- Allen Klein

Chapter 1: Drawing Materials

Pencils

You will most likely want to draw your rough sketches with a pencil first. They are normally erasable, easy to find and affordable. Two main types of pencils to use are graphite pencils (the one you can sharpen) and mechanical or clutch pencils. Graphite pencils are very versatile and varies from "hard" (2H - 9H) and grey to soft and "black" (B - B9). HB pencils are good for general-purpose because they are not as hard as "H" and not as black as "B". To avoid smudging when you want to colour, use harder pencils. If you want to do your fashion illustration only with graphite pencil, you might want to use three or four pencils of different hardness.

Some people may prefer clutch pencils since it produces a constant line thickness and doesn't require sharpening. The standard lead used for clutch pencils ranges from 0,5 mm to 2 mm. ▼

HB pencil

Clutch pencil

Blue clutch pencil

Paper

The paper surface you choose will depend on the medium that you are going to work with. Hot press paper is very smooth and is preferable for clean pencil lines and erasing. Standard 80gsm printer paper is sufficient for sketching with pencil and is very affordable. This kind of paper does, however, disintegrate and warp with more intensive artistic processes. Cold press paper has a coarse tooth (texture), it is preferred for watercolours and is suitable for most mediums. Generally paper intended specifically for watercolours and alcohol markers also work well for most other mediums.

Bristol board is a heavy paper and extremely versatile. It has a smooth finish and is ideal for either sketching with pencil, inking or when working with watercolour paint or alcohol markers.

Chapter 1: Drawing Materials

Erasers

Erasers are necessary when you want to erase your drawing mistakes. It can also be used for blending and "lifting off" pigments to imitate highlights. The types of erasers that are recommended are gum erasers, clutch erasers and putty erasers. Gum erasers are very soft, do not smear much and do not damage paper easily. Clutch erasers are for precision erasing, especially for creating highlights or "drawing" textures by erasing "negative" lines. Putty erasers are malleable and soft and are more suited to lifting materials such as charcoal and pastel. Plastic erasers tend to smear sketches and are not best suited for fashion illustration. ▼

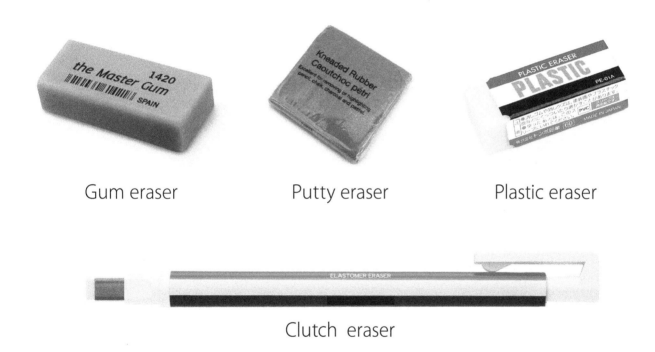

Gum eraser   Putty eraser   Plastic eraser

Clutch eraser

Sharpeners

Keep your pencil lines neat and fine by sharpening your pencils with a good sharpener or utility knife. Pencil shavings can also be used for blend effects using cotton wool or a que tip. ▶

Chapter 1: Drawing Materials

Pen & Inks

Inking is when you trace over your pencil lines with ink to make the lines bold and clean. Inking the fashion illustration is not always necessary, but can add extra definition. The types of pens that you can use are dip pens, technical pens, ballpoint pen and fineliners. Dip pens require dipping into ink and allow you to vary the line width. Technical pens or fineliners are easier to use and produce consistent lines. They do, however, need to be cleaned regularly. Fineliners are often used for technical drawings, especially those with thicknesses of 0,1 mm and 0,5 mm. ▼

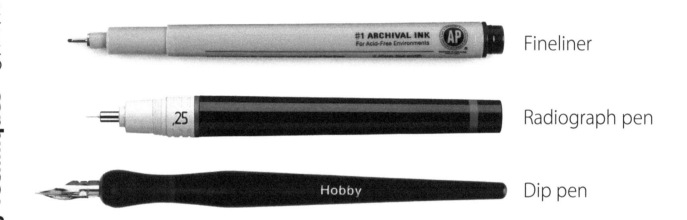

Fineliner

Radiograph pen

Dip pen

Water Based Marker

The dye of these markers is carried by a solution of water or a combination of glycerin and water. Water based markers may generally not perform as well as alcohol based markers. You may need to add water to blend the dye. School-grade markers are usually water based and not suitable for creating transparent layering of colours. Nevertheless, they do normally work fine for some more solid colour rendering. For your solid colour rendering, (for example primary red or blue) it is advised to buy water based markers instead of alcohol based markers. They are more cost effective and very similar to performing the same task when it comes to solid colours. ▶

Chapter 1: Drawing Materials

Alcohol Based Marker

The dye in alcohol based markers are suspended in alcohol and therefore fast drying. They are usually double-sided with different nibs for different purposes. They are refillable and their nibs are replaceable. Unlike water based markers, these markers create a translucent effect similar to watercolour paint.

What makes alcohol based markers so popular among fashion illustrators are their ability to blend to create a smooth gradient. You can further blend colours of different hues with an alcohol based colourless blender fluid or markers. You can use these colourless blending markers in combination with other mediums such as watercolour pencils and water-based markers. ▼

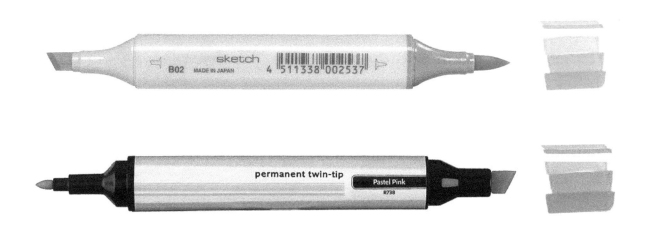

Brushes

Good quality sable brushes are your best choice if you are going to use watercolours or watercolour pencils for your fashion illustration. It can additionally be used to ink the fashion illustration after colouring (with black ink), to add definition. You will probably use round brush heads for inking and fine detail and flat brush heads for colouring. ▼

Chapter 1: Drawing Materials

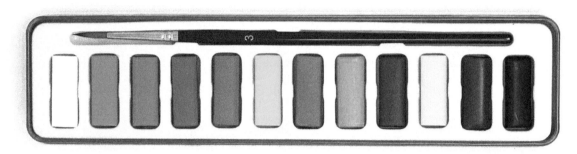

Watercolour Paint

▲ Watercolour paint either normally comes in pans that needs to be brushed with wet brushes, or tubes containing moist paint. Lighter shades are created by diluting the paint with water. You will have to leave areas open to represent white, or you can use masking fluid to block the pigment to create white areas. Watercolour paint is translucent and not as opaque as acrylic paint. Many fashion designers/illustrators prefer this effect for their style of illustrations. ▶

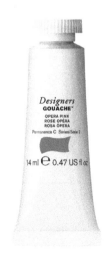 

Acrylic and Gouache Paint

◀ Both gouache and acrylic paint are soluble in water. Because both types of paint are opaque and produce solid colours, the whites can be used to correct mistakes and to create highlights. Acrylic paint normally produces brighter colours than gouache.

Chapter 1: Drawing Materials

Watercolour Pencils & Colour Pencils

◀ Both regular and watercolour pencils can be used for layering and blending. Colour pencils do not mix with water and it takes considerably longer to cover areas, which can result in white gaps.

Watercolour pencil marks appear like normal colour pencils, but the pigment spreads when water is added or when using a colourless blender marker. The resulting effect appears similar to watercolour paint and is also easier to use.

Watercolour pencils can also be used in combination with watercolour paint.

Colourless Blender

The blender is an inkless alcohol marker used to blend ink of different colours or shades. It can be used to wet a large area of paper before applying ink. In addition, it can be used to blend watercolour pencils. ▼

Masking Fluid

Masking fluid is used for creating highlights, fabric texture and patterns. It resists paint when painted over and leaves a white area after peeling it away. Masking fluid dries quickly and should ideally be applied with a brush which needs to be cleaned afterwards. ▶

Chapter 1: Drawing Materials

Tracing Paper

If you don't have a light box, you can use tracing paper to sketch your rough drawings onto. When you place tracing paper over a drawing or croquis, it will show through the tracing paper and serve as another "layer" for you to sketch your rough drawings over.

French Curves

French curves were traditionally used to draw necklines, sleeves, bust and waist variations. They were especially effective for drawing neat curved lines for technical drawings.

It might be good for a fashion design student to practise using a french curve to appreciate how designers in the past have done it. For some designers, the use of french curves have become irrelevant, since it is easier and quicker to draw curves with computer software. ▶

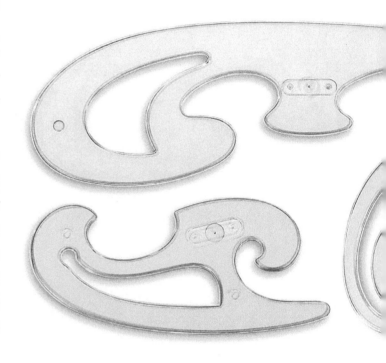

Flexible Curve

This is a handy tool for drawing technical flats, since it can be manipulated into large or small curves.

Some can be used for measuring curves and is furthermore used for pattern drafting. ▶

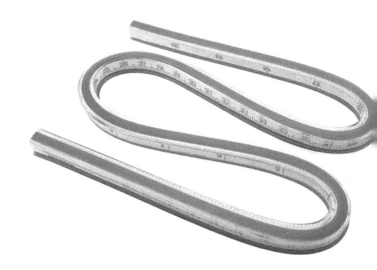

Chapter 2:
Design Elements & Principles

Formal elements are applied in many creative industries such as the visual arts, graphic design, architecture and interior design (to name a few). The use of these elements provokes either a strong or subliminal response in the viewer or the wearer. When these elements are applied well, it forms the basis of good drawing and design.

These **formal elements** are: line, texture, space, tonal value, form, shape and colour.

The basic elements of design are applied in ways that are called principles.

These **design principles** are: balance, unity, repetition, rhythm, proportion, contrast, emphasis and movement.

For the fashion designer it is essential to have an understanding of what the formal elements and design principles are, and how to apply it.

Primary

"The hardest thing in fashion is not to be known for a logo, but to be known for a silhouette."
- Giambattista Valli

Chapter 2: Design Elements & Principles

Formal Elements

Line

As in fine art, the line drawing is the foundation of the fashion illustration. Line can be explained in terms of the stroke variation you apply when drawing, but also how you demonstrate lines in the actual design. The most common use of lines in a garment is the use of seamlines. Folds, gathers and darts are some of the decorative detail that also create lines. Line can be used to emphasise or disguise and to draw attention to or away from a certain part. Vertical lines have a slimming effect and create the illusion of length (e.g. princess style lines and pencil striped skirts). Horizontal lines draw attention to the width of the body.

Tonal value

In terms of the fashion illustration, tonal value can be understood as how dark or light you want an object to be, by adding black or white tone. When you want to create dimension and depth in your illustration, you will use tonal values to depict light and shadow. You can create darker or lighter colour gradients for shading or highlighting by adding black or white to that one colour.

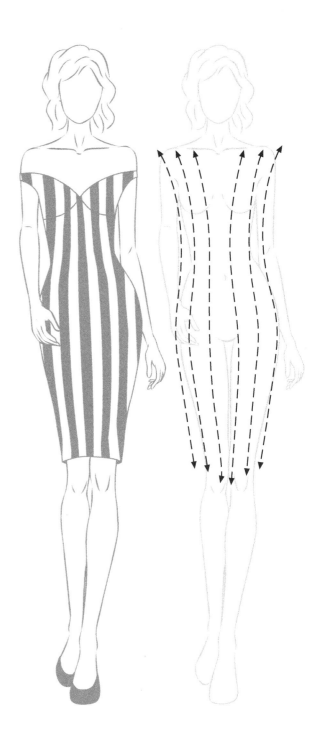

▲ The effect of line on the appearance of the body.

Chapter 2: Design Elements & Principles

▲ The effect of space on the appearance of the body.

Texture

Fabric texture has a visual as well as a tactile component. How fabric fibres are woven or knitted influences the texture and weight of the fabric. Fabrics can be smooth and matte, smooth and shiny (satin) or textured and shiny (velvet).

Many designers want to be inspired by the fabric texture and properties before they start sketching designs. Designers need to understand how fabric of different weights and textures behave to be able to pair the design with the correct fabric.

The weight and degree of stiffness of the fabric will influence how it drapes on the body and what type of garment it should be used for. Light weight fabric such as silks and chiffons, may be more suited for dresses, whereas a stiff fabrics such as denim, may be more suited for pants and jackets.

Space

This can be understood as the area around or between the focal point, or different elements in the illustration or design. A dress can have a floral pattern either densely arranged, or in a more spaciously distributed manner. Each will have a different visual effect to your fashion illustration or garment.

Fashion Illustration Drawing Techniques © Mila Markle

Chapter 2: Design Elements & Principles

Shape, Silhouette and Form

Most objects in existence comprises of basic shapes. It is important to have an elementary understanding of basic shapes to be able to draw any object. The element of shape can also be understood as shapes that are used in the design itself. Shape contributes toward the silhouette of the design.

Whether you are sketching rough drawings of your designs or the figure for your fashion illustration, you will be incorporating basic shapes. Knowing how to shade and render the basic shapes such as a cylinder for instance, will help you to know how to shade and render the folds of a dress. It will also enable you to understand where to render the shadows and highlights of the curvature of human anatomy. ▼

Square   Sphere/Circle   Cylinder   Triangle

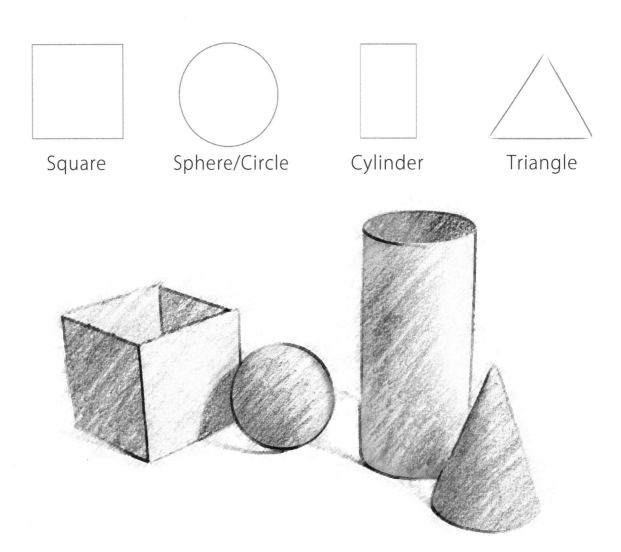

Chapter 2: Design Elements & Principles

Silhouette can be regarded as the first recognizable shape or outline of a garment that you see. The silhouette of a garment is also seen as form because garments are three-dimensional. There have been many different types of silhouettes through the different fashion eras. Here are some of the most common silhouettes of the modern age. ▼

Classically
Waisted

Empire

Sheath/Skinny

Mermaid

Hourglass

Tent

Asymmetrical

Column

Fashion Illustration Drawing Techniques

Chapter 2: Design Elements & Principles

Fashion Illustration Drawing Techniques © Mila Markle

Colour

Aside from the silhouette, colour is pretty much the first thing you notice when looking at a garment. Colour has characteristics such as: hue, value and saturation. The colour wheel is a simple colour system that is based on the three primary colours/hues: Red, Blue and Yellow. These hues are mixed to get the secondary and tertiary colours. ▼

Blue + Yellow = Green
Blue + Red = Purple
Red + Yellow = Orange

Primary colours are mixed with secondary colours to get tertiary colours. Before designing a collection for a specific season, most designers may first research which colours may be trending. The change in colour trends can be according to colour temperature (warmer/cooler), value (lighter/darker), intensity or hue (e.g. red or yellow).

The colour wheel enables designers to choose colour schemes to elicit certain desired responses from the viewer, to create visual interest, direct attention to a specific part and to create a sense of unity. These colour schemes have been named:

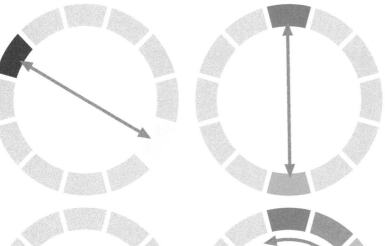

◀ Complementary: Colours that oppose each other e.g. red and green or purple and yellow.

◀ Adjacent colours: 2 to 4 colours next to each other.

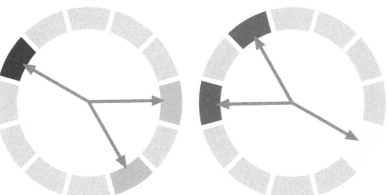

◀ Split-Complementary

Fashion Illustration Drawing Techniques © *Mila Markle*

Chapter 2: Design Elements & Principles

Design Principles

Whether doing a fashion illustration or planning the design, the design principles should also be kept in mind:

Balance: When there is symmetry on both sides there is balance.

Harmony: Using fabrics or colours that create unity.

Repetition: Certain design elements are applied more than once.

Rhythm: The pattern created by repeating elements in a certain way.

Proportion: This should be considered when drawing the figure and when designing a garment. For example, take into consideration how big is a certain part (of the body or garment) in relation to another.

Contrast: Distinction between colours or textures can draw attention.

Emphasis: Using formal elements or principles to create a focal point in a garment. Anything that can draw attention, such as contrasting colours or a belt, can create a focal point.

Movement: Directing the viewer's eyes along a certain path, by using rhythm, creates a sense of movement. This is also demonstrated by whether the fabric is flowing or more rigid.

As with art, it would be of benefit to designers to practise some restraint when deciding which of the elements and principles to apply. Too many dramatic elements and principles used together might be visually overwhelming. Imagine an exaggerated hourglass silhouette (ball gown) with many ruffles in very bright neon colours. It is like mixing too many ingredients for something that should only need a few in order to be great.

Chapter 2: Design Elements & Principles

Applying the formal elements and design principles:

Every design/illustration will usually have more than one element. You will find it difficult to design anything without colour, silhouette or line.

The design principles do not necessarily have to be applied all at once. These principles are, however, interconnected and the use of one can influence how another principle is used. The elements and principles of design can be applied to just a single design or to a whole collection. A successful collection will be unified by repetition, while there should also be variety to keep it interesting.

The fashion designer should decide which principles will be used together to create the ideal effect.

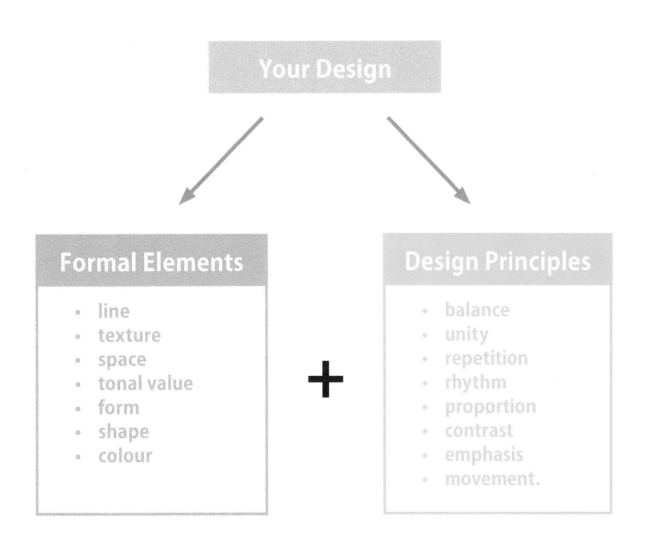

Your Design

Formal Elements

- line
- texture
- space
- tonal value
- form
- shape
- colour

+

Design Principles

- balance
- unity
- repetition
- rhythm
- proportion
- contrast
- emphasis
- movement.

Chapter 2: Design Elements & Principles

Example 1

In this outfit the colour and stripes in the pants are repeated in the top. Contrast is created by the colours. Texture is represented by the fabric (mesh) of the lower part of the top. Line is represented by the stripes of the fabric as well as the seamlines.

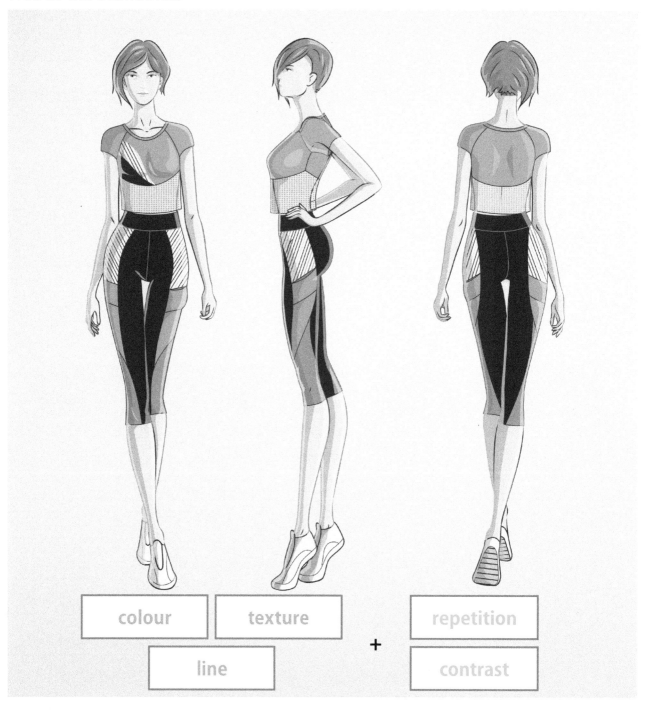

colour	texture		repetition
line		**+**	contrast

Chapter 2: Design Elements & Principles

Example 2

The use of texture can be seen in the top part of the dress. The Folds/pleats in the skirt repeats and create rhythm and movement. Movement is also created by the flowing nature of the fabric. The colours of the bodice and skirt creates harmony.

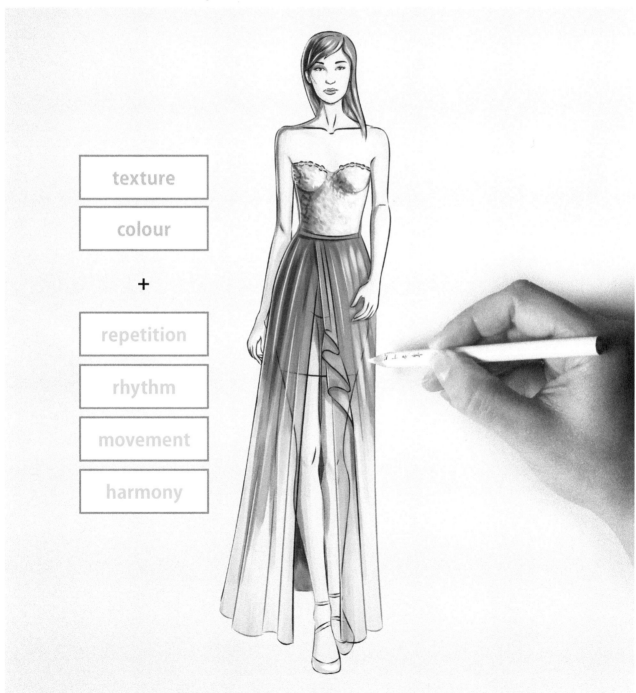

texture

colour

+

repetition

rhythm

movement

harmony

Chapter 2: Design Elements & Principles

Example 3

There is repetition of the design element in the top and skirt as well as between the two outfits. If these outfits form part of a collection, the repetition of colour will create unity.

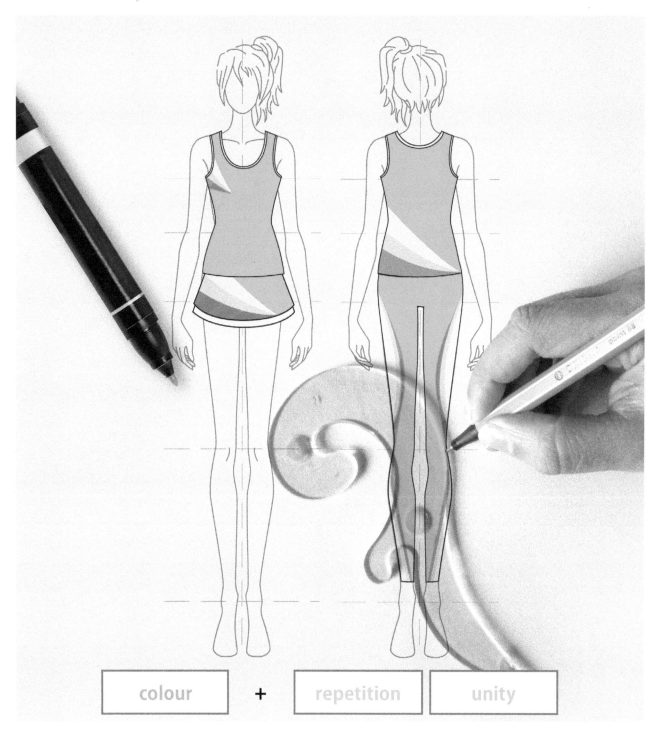

colour	+	repetition	unity

Chapter 3:
Roughs & Technical Flats

In this chapter, you will be shown how to use croquis templates for your rough sketches as well as technical drawings (by using some examples).

The aim of rough drawings is to conceptualize and plan your designs and to stimulate your creativity. Roughs are normally drawn in a loose and expressive manner without wasting too much time in the process.

Croquis templates with dotted lines can be used to create the technical drawing, which is the next step. Technical drawings, also known as "technical flats", are 2-dimensional symmetrical drawings of the front and back of a garment and features important construction details and annotations.

"What you wear is how you present yourself to the world, especially today, when human contacts are so quick. Fashion is instant language"
- Miuccia Prada

Chapter 3: Roughs & Technical Flats

When sketching your roughs, it helps to have a croquis template to provide a guideline for the borders of your design. It will also help you to draw more **proportionately correct**.

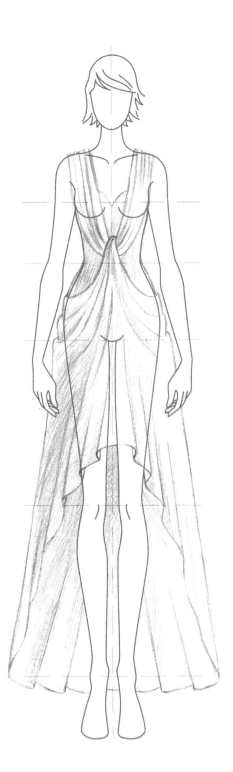

To work in layers, you can use tracing paper and place it over the page, or draw with a different colour pencil, to help you distinguish between the lines. You can also use a light box (light table) to work in layers.

If you want to design a specific garment for a specific occasion, the ideal is to sketch as many roughs as possible, and then choose the best one.

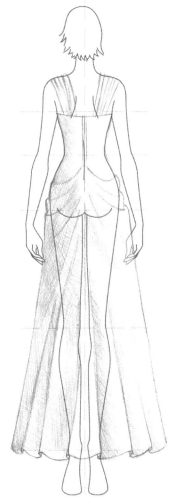

Chapter 3: Roughs & Technical Flats

The technical drawing serves as a **blueprint** or map of the design for the pattern makers and seamstresses. The annotations in this image indicate detail such as top stitching, the different types of fabric used and so forth. ▼

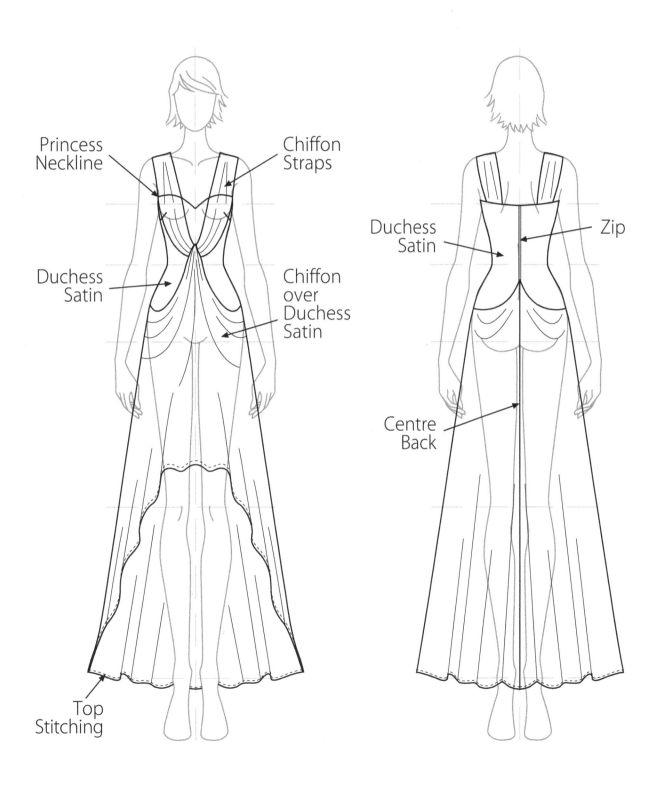

Princess Neckline

Chiffon Straps

Duchess Satin

Chiffon over Duchess Satin

Top Stitching

Duchess Satin

Zip

Centre Back

Fashion Illustration Drawing Techniques © *Mila Markle*

The technical flat is drawn more neatly than the rough drawings. If you are drawing your technical flat by hand, the use of french curves will be of great use to create smooth lines. Care should be taken to draw it symmetrically, except if the design is asymmetrical.

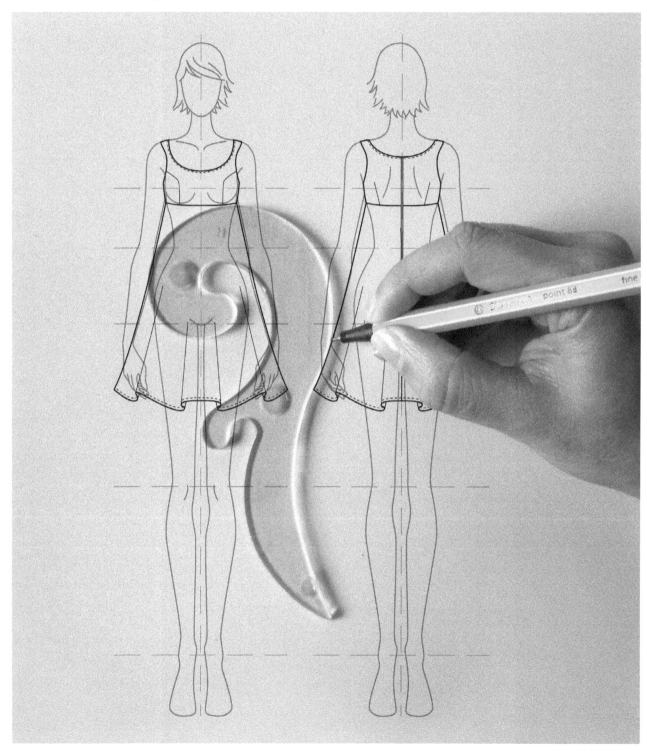

Fashion Illustration Drawing Techniques © *Mila Markle*

Chapter 3: Roughs & Technical Flats

Vertical line   Horizontal line

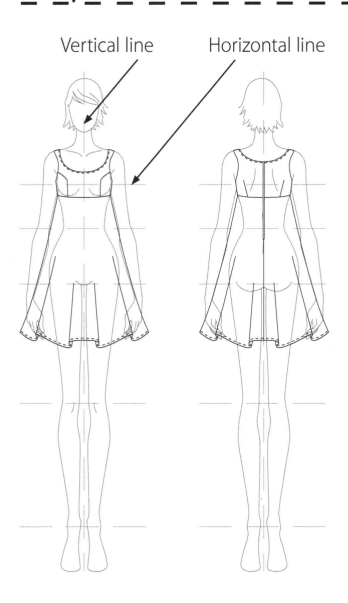

▲ The vertical centre line is there to enable you to draw symmetrical to the vertical axis. The horizontal lines are there to indicate the important landmarks as well as to help with symmetry. Make sure that your design will be practical to construct.

Consider whether the wearer will be able to get in and out of the outfit through a zip or button stand.

Chapter 3: Roughs & Technical Flats

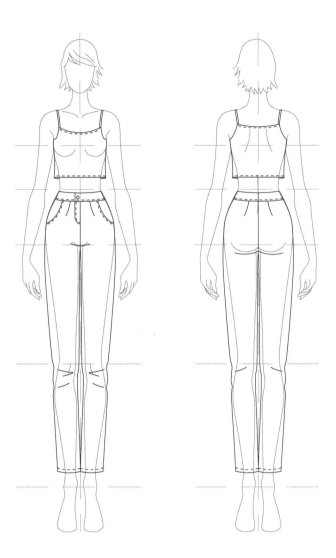

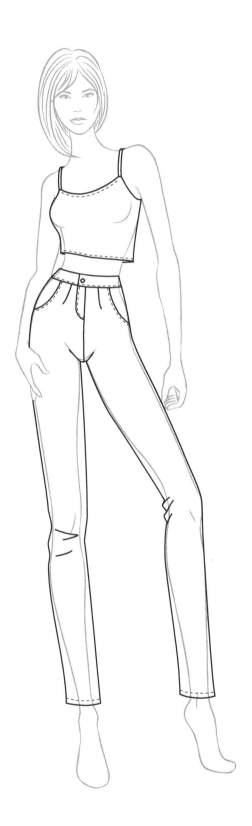

▲ The technical flat should contain important detail that indicate to the pattern maker and seamstress how the garment should be constructed.

Indicate on your technical flat where a **zip** and other details such as **darts**, **buttons**, **pockets**, and **top stitching** will be.

Chapter 3: Roughs & Technical Flats

Fashion Illustration Drawing Techniques © *Mila Markle*

▲ If drawn by hand, a fineliner of 0,5 mm can be used for drawing the outline of the silhouette and important seamlines.

Finer detail such as top stitching and folds can be indicated with 0,1 mm lines.

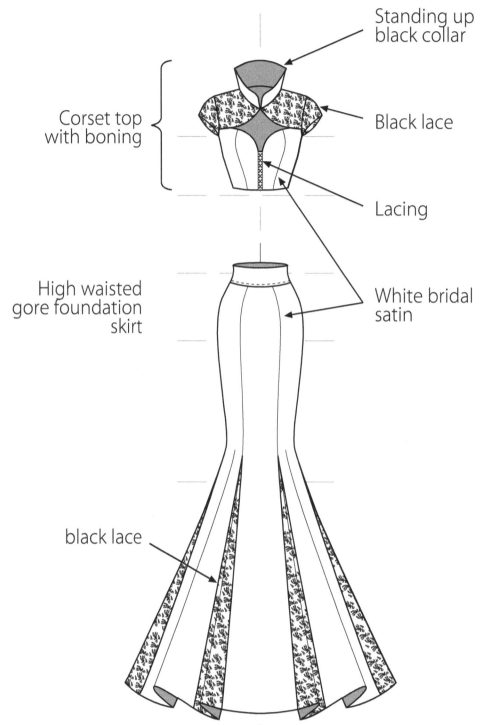

Standing up
black collar

Corset top
with boning

Black lace

Lacing

High waisted
gore foundation
skirt

White bridal
satin

black lace

▲ Here is a technical flat of a garment which will be discussed and illustrated later on. This is a formal wear garment, consisting of a corset top with boning and a high waisted gore foundation skirt. The black lace parts have been indicated with a graphical pattern. Other features include top stitching. The grey areas indicate the inside of the garment

Fashion Illustration Drawing Techniques © *Mila Markle*

Chapter 3: Roughs & Technical Flats

More examples of technical flats:

Whether the fabric you choose has a stretch factor or not, will determine whether a zip or functioning button stand might be necessary. A dress made from a non-stretch fabric will also need darts (contouring) to fit to the shape of the body. ▶

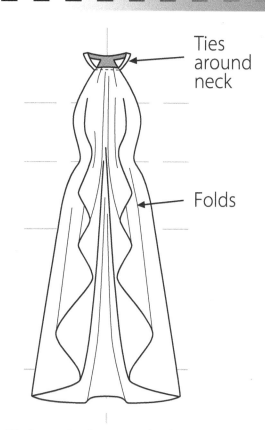

Ties around neck

Folds

Tafetta halter-neck dress

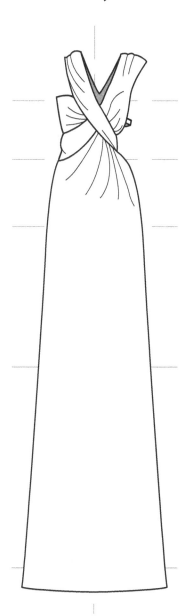

Stretch crepe draped dress

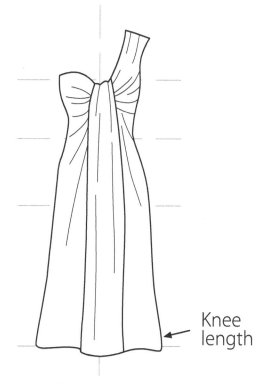

Knee length

Asymmetric draped satin dress

Chapter 3: Roughs & Technical Flats

The same steps of roughs and technical flats can be followed for male fashion with the help of male croquis. ▼

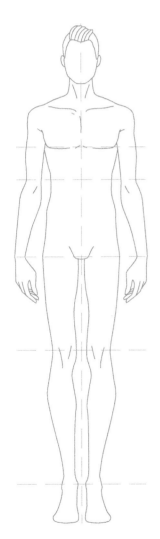

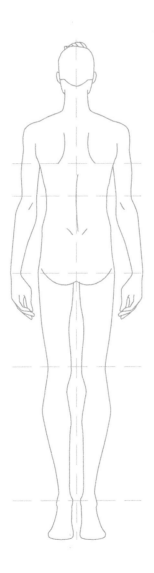

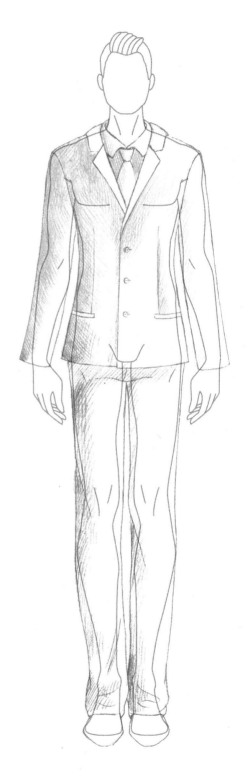

Chapter 3: Roughs & Technical Flats

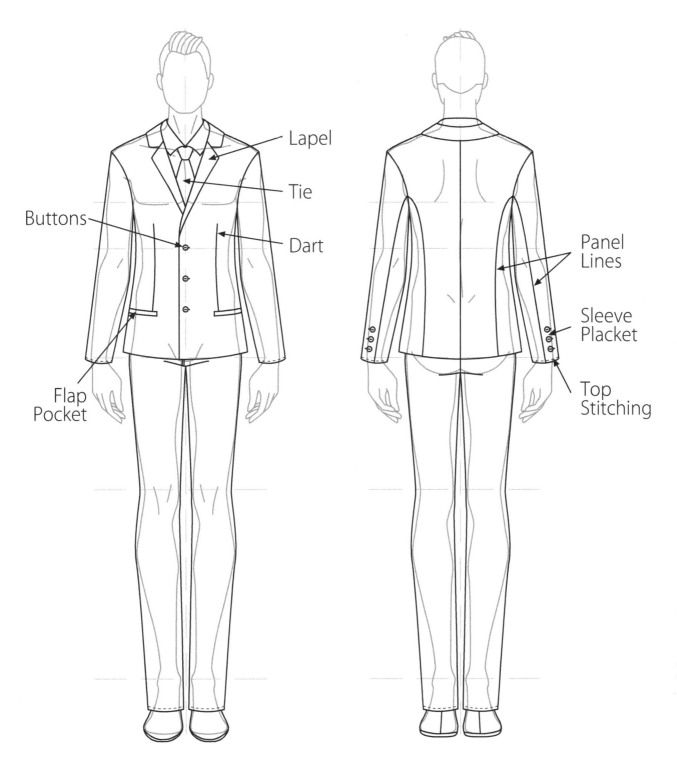

Lapel

Tie

Dart

Buttons

Flap
Pocket

Panel
Lines

Sleeve
Placket

Top
Stitching

Fashion Illustration Drawing Techniques © Mila Markle

35

Chapter 4: Rendering Techniques

As a fashion designer or illustrator, you need to express or illustrate to the viewer the fabric that you have in mind for the design. It is important to capture the colour, texture, weight and reflectiveness of the desired fabric in a convincing yet loose way.

The most important aspects to consider when rendering or colouring the fashion illustration are:

- Art medium
- Fabric texture
- Direction of the light source

When rendering your fashion illustration, you will have to choose the direction of the light source. Certain fabrics, such as silk, reflect light more than others. When colouring a shiny dress with folds, consider where to shade and to illustrate the shine of the fabric with highlights.

"In order to be irreplaceable one must always be different."
- Coco Chanel

Chapter 4: Rendering Techniques

Watercolour Pencil

The most common way to use watercolour pencil is to colour with dry pencil on dry paper and add water with a brush to blend. You can blend the dry pencil markings as you want and use an eraser when still dry. It might be better to start with a lighter colour first.

When you add water, the colours will become brighter and blend more. It might be easier to control how the colours blend by using a colourless blender marker. Although alcohol markers will also work well, they will influence the outcome of the colour due to the pigment they contain. The same principle as regular watercolour paints can be used: colour on a separate piece of paper and transfer the pigment to your sketch with a wet brush or the tip of a blender. You can press a wet brush to the pencil tip and transfer the pigment to your sketch.

Dry pencil on wet paper

Wet pencil on dry paper

Wet brush on wet paper

Dry pencil on dry paper

Layering

Two-pencil gradient

Watercolour Paint

Watercolour paint is often favoured by illustrators/artists for it's unique transparent qualities.

Because watercolour is transparent, applying one colour over another, will form a new colour. This technique is known as **layering** or **glazing**.

If you are using watercolour pans, use a brush to transfer the chosen colour to a palette. Using a palette for mixing will prevent you from contaminating your colour pans. On the palette, you can mix different colours and add more water to dilute the colours. Avoid contaminating pans by rinsing brushes before using another colour.

Oftentimes a colour wash needs to be done - this is the first layer of colour that serves as the foundation. It is easier to work from light to dark than from dark to light. It is therefore better to do a light colour wash first which you can build on gradually.

Two-colour layering

Multiple-colour layering

Chapter 4: Rendering Techniques

Blending can be achieved by the wet on dry or wet on wet technique. Wet on dry is painting with a wet brush onto dry paper. With this technique you have to wait for the paint to dry before applying the next brush stroke. If you want to blend with this technique, you should use a clean damp brush to spread the pigment.

Wet on wet technique is painting with a wet brush onto wet paper. With this technique, the colours flow into each other and blends more easily. Certain effects can only be achieved by using the wet on wet technique.

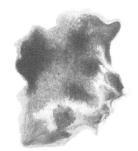

Wet on dry   Wet on wet

If you want an area to have a uniform colour, you will do a flat wash. This is more easily done with the wet on dry technique. The flat wash is done by moving a "paint bead" downward with horizontal brush strokes and tilting the paper slightly.

A gradient effect is achieved by diluting the colour more and more as you move down the paper. This is called a gradient wash and is easier to do with the wet on wet technique. A two-tone gradient wash is similar to a flat or graded wash but is done by blending two different colours.

Flat wash   Gradient   Two-tone
                     wash   gradient wash

Chapter 4: Rendering Techniques

Here is an example of a male fashion figure rendered with various watercolour techniques. The finer details are touched up with a black radiograph pen. ▼

The texture and weight of fabric will determine which medium you might prefer to use.

Chapter 4: Rendering Techniques

Alcohol Markers

Whether you are colouring skin or a garment, you will create better shading and definition by working with three shades of the same colour or colour range. When you have chosen a colour, get a version that is 2-3 shades lighter and a version that is 2-3 shades darker. It is also recommended to get 3 shades of grey for adding extra definition.

2 colour blending
with 4 tonal difference

2 colour blending
with 2 tonal difference

3 colour blending
with 2 tonal difference

2 layers

3 layers

Chapter 4: Rendering Techniques

Rendering Texture

The dry brush technique can be used to illustrate the texture of something such as fur or feathers. This technique simply involves applying paint with a dry brush. The texture of your paper will help determine the textures you generate when lightly stroking your brush. This is also known as **scumbling**.

Additionally, fur or feathers can be illustrated by using a dabbing technique. This is done by dabbing the brush repeatedly to create darker spots over lighter areas. ▶

Scumbling　　　Dabbing

Rendering Matte Fabric

One way of creating highlights is by the "**lifting off**" technique. This entails removing paint from the paper with a clean, damp brush. This will work well for illustrating matte fabrics. Details can then be added by using pencils or markers. ▶

Chapter 4: Rendering Techniques

Rendering Reflective Fabrics

To illustrate shiny fabrics such as silk, you will have to create highlights. A strong contrast between light and shadows is necessary to illustrate a high shine. Make sure to establish the direction of the light source. The best way to achieve bright highlights or shapes with watercolour paint or watercolour pencil, is by reserving white. This can be achieved by leaving areas without pigment (paint or marker ink), or by using masking fluid to achieve hard edges.

You can also use white acrylic paint, gouache or correction fluid to illustrate the reflections on fabrics such as silk. A white colour pencil will similarly work for some instances of drawing highlights. ▼

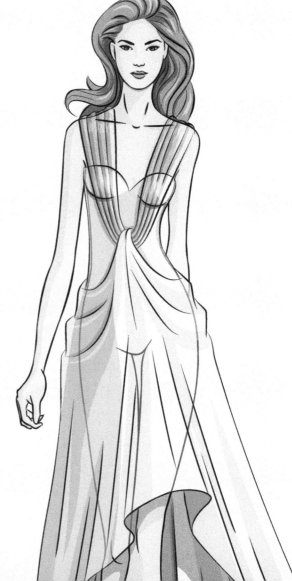

Chapter 4: Rendering Techniques

Rendering, inking and colouring your pencil sketches

One of the fastest ways to bring life to your fashion illustrations, is to work directly over your actual pencil sketches. ▼

▲ Pencils

▲ Inks over pencils

▲ Colours

You can use an array of drawing media to achieve this. When doing this, it is important to use good quality paper or bristol board. This is so that your illustrations can withstand the multiple mediums as well as not warp when applying water. Watercolour pencils can be used to colour certain parts so that when you apply water, it will blend into a watercolour feel. When different colours of pencils are used over each other, the water will mix the colours to create even more colour variants.

Watercolour paint and guache is another option to use directly over your pencils. Either can be diluted so that when you work over your sketches, the pencil drawing will still be visible. In some instances, you may want to draw your inks in the last stage in order to prevent the ink from dissolving.

Alcohol markers and alcohol blending pens are highly recommended for fashion illustration. Alcohol blending pens contain no colour pigment. They will "smudge" or "blend" graphite pencils, and especially watercolour pencils, to create very effective rendering without greatly affecting the original colours used. Alcohol markers has a similar effect, except that they contain colour pigment. They too can blend pencils to some lesser extent, but they are also very effective to use as a standalone tool to render fashion illustrations. They are especially effective to use over your original graphite pencils and inks.

Fashion Illustration Drawing Techniques

Chapter 4: Rendering Techniques

Example 1

Whichever medium you choose for this approach, you can define your illustrations by using various types of black fineliners or radiograph pens. ▼

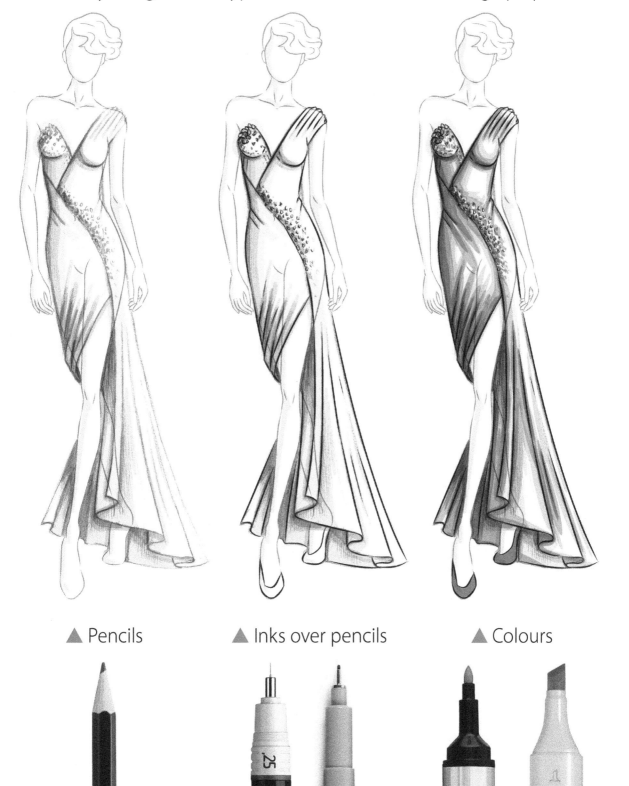

▲ Pencils   ▲ Inks over pencils   ▲ Colours

Fashion Illustration Drawing Techniques © *Mila Markle*

45

Chapter 4: Rendering Techniques

Example 2

▲ Pencils   ▲ Inks over pencils   ▲ Colours

Fashion Illustration Drawing Techniques © *Mila Markle*

46

Chapter 4: Rendering Techniques

Example 3

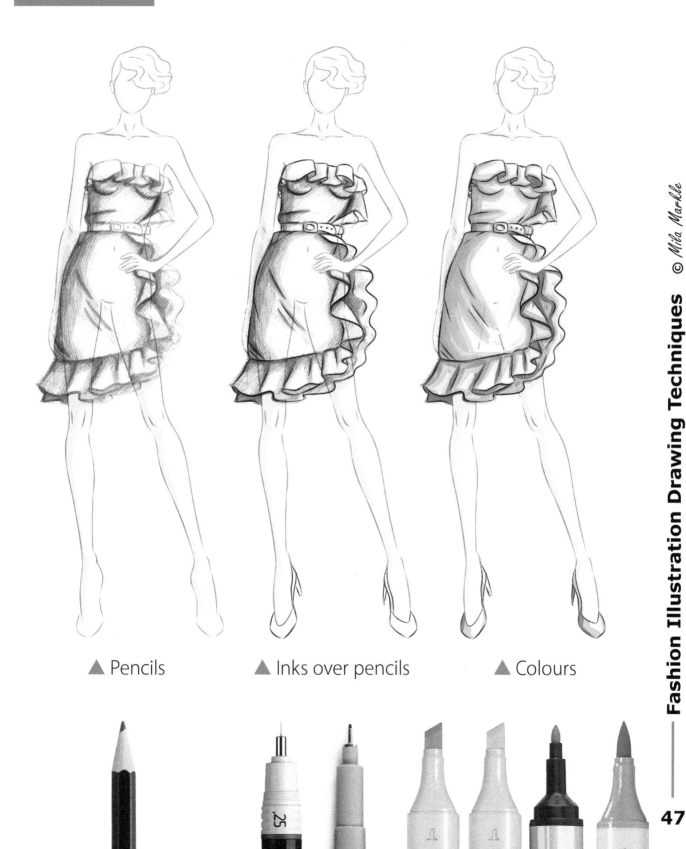

▲ Pencils　　　　▲ Inks over pencils　　　　▲ Colours

Fashion Illustration Drawing Techniques　© *Mila Marble*

Rendering Sheer Fabrics

With sheer (see-through) fabrics, such as chiffon, tulle or lace, you will need to illustrate the skin that is visible underneath the fabric. You simply have to understand the concept of working with layers. A sheer fabric that is darker than the skin tone will be the easiest to illustrate. A lighter chiffon will require of you to give an extra layer of colour to the surrounding exposed skin or that you render the exposed skin separately to the covered skin.

When rendering fabric over the skin tone with coloured pencils, the result will be a mixture of different coloured dots because of the textured paper. This will create the optical effect of transparent fabric as well.

You can start with inking the pencil lines first, or you can do it last depending on your preference (each approach has different results). ▼

Materials needed ▼

Chapter 4: Rendering Techniques

The sleeves, the part covering the shoulders as well as the triangular shaped panels at the bottom will represent black lace. The rest of the top and the skirt will represent a solid fabric. ▼

The same steps to illustrate chiffon fabric can be used to illustrate lace. The only difference will be the floral detail that will be added to the lace. Adding the floral detail will make it distinguishable as most commonly found lace. Being a light colour, the skin is rendered first.

After rendering the skin, the hair and face is coloured (as they are darker in tone). The shoes and the collar are made black to tie in with the black lace and the floral pattern details that will follow in the latter steps.

▲ The colour of the fabric is applied over the skin layer so that the skin is still visible. The bottom lace panels are rendered next.

The flesh is directly in contact with the top lace part, but not with the bottom lace panels. Because the rest of the dress is white, shading is done only with grey. ▶

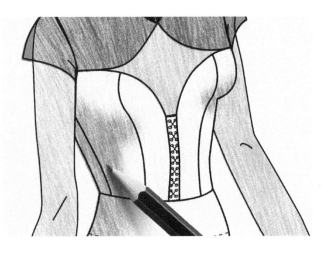

Chapter 4: Rendering Techniques

Take note that shading should follow the shape of the body and that shadows fall underneath curves such as the breasts. More shading is applied to the dress for definition and shading is added to the flesh with a darker colour. You can demonstrate shadows on the skin covered by the lace with a darker skin tone, grey or a darker tone of the sheer fabric.

Highlights are applied next with a white colour pencil or white pastel pencil, where the light would fall. You can also use an eraser to lift-off colour (if you have used colour pencil). Highlights can be achieved through many ways depending on which medium you are working with. ▼

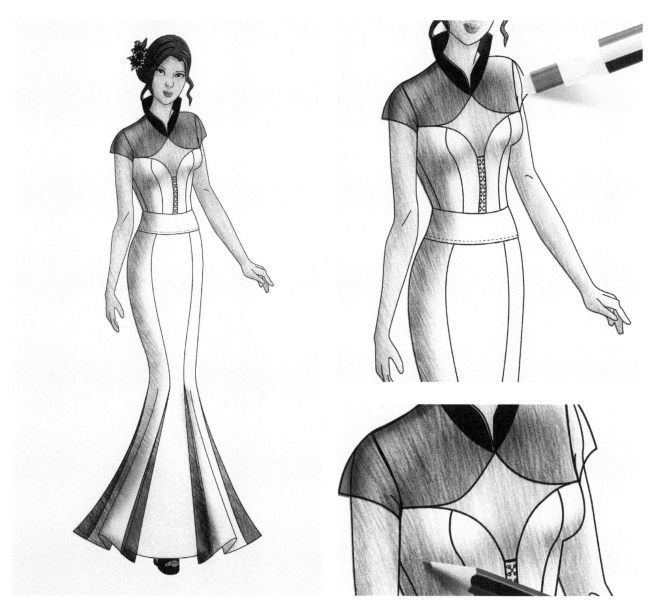

Chapter 4: Rendering Techniques

Reflected light (a second source of light) is done on the same side as the shadows. Reflected light is also often light reflected from surfaces onto an object. This effect can be achieved by also using a colour pencil or pastel pencil. ▼

▲

In this last step the detail is added to make the fabric to be distinguishable as lace. The floral pattern inking can be done with solid black (with fineliner, a technical pen or black marker).

Chapter 4: Rendering Techniques

Fashion Illustration Drawing Techniques © *Mila Markle*

Chapter 5:
The Fashion Illustration

In this Chapter, you will be shown step-by-step examples how fashion figure templates can be used in conjunction with your own illustrations. This method speeds up the process in order to create effective fashion illustrations. These templates makes it easy for you to start designing clothes and to draw and colour immediately.

When you are creating the fashion illustration, keep in mind that the pose of the figure and accessories should be carefully chosen to be consistent with the specific mood that you have in mind.

Traditionally, fashion figures are drawn up to nine to ten heads tall. If you want to draw your own fashion figure, try to stick to a certain amount of head lengths. Remember that measurements can vary from artist to artist. ▶

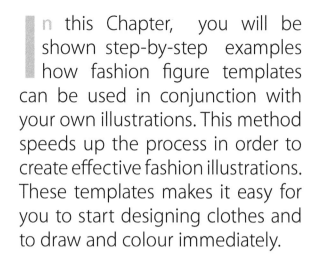

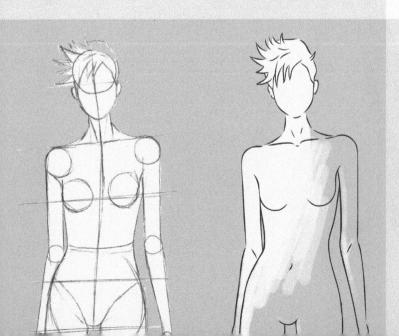

"The dress must follow the body of a woman, not the body following the shape of the dress."
- Hubert de Givenchy

Chapter 5: The Fashion Illustration

If you prefer drawing your own figures but are unfamiliar with it, starting with gesture drawing is recommended. Gesture drawing is the same as drawing stick figures, and will generate the pose of the figure. Your figure should not appear to be falling over but has to be drawn in a balanced way. Keep in mind that the centre line runs through the weight bearing leg, when standing or walking. You should be able to draw a vertical line through the joints on the weight bearing side, meaning they should be aligned.

Although fashion figures are drawn in a very exaggerated way, there is still a degree of proportion. If you want to draw your figures proportionately correct, a useful way is to use the head length as a unit of measurement. This is known as the "canon of proportion" and is commonly used in other artistic disciplines.

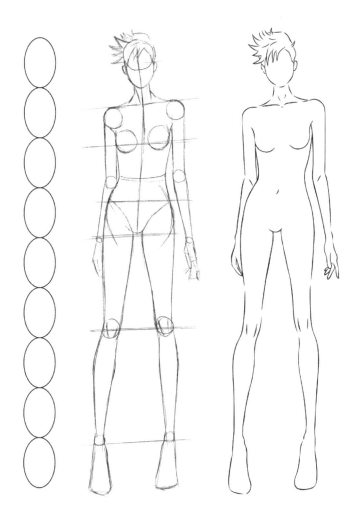

◀ Unlike typical human figure drawing, which uses 8 heads for proportion, fashion figures can be drawn using 9 heads.

Chapter 5: The Fashion Illustration

Example 1

When you have decided on the design you want to use, start drawing it over your fashion figure with a pencil. You can use graphite pencil or blue pencil.

Decide on whether you want a walking pose or a standing pose. A walking pose might have more of a striking effect and simulate that of a runway pose. ▶

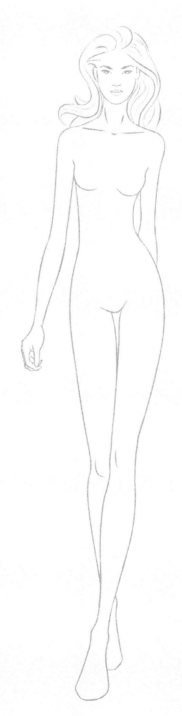

Chapter 5: The Fashion Illustration

Because the fashion figure is not symmetrical like the croquis, consider how the garment will drape and move with the body. This figure is walking, so it will mean that the clothing should not be static.

Fabric is stretched over a bony prominence, such as the shoulder, and will create folds over body parts that is bent such as an elbow or knee. ▶

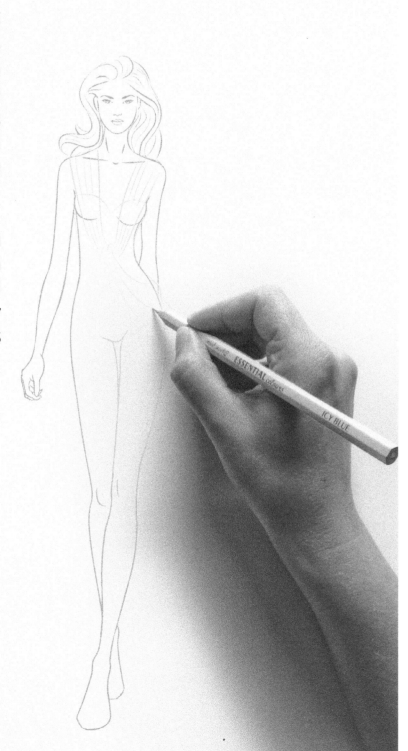

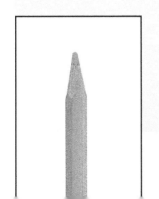

Chapter 5: The Fashion Illustration

The dress is drawn in a manner that shows how it moves with the figure. Drawing folds suggests that fabric is gathered or that there is excess fabric draped around an object or body. The folds around the hips are drape folds that form a "U" shape, like the folds you see in a cloak.

When you are satisfied with the line drawing, you can start rendering. ▶

Chapter 5: The Fashion Illustration

The skin is rendered first keeping in mind that transparent fabric will be rendered over the figure at a later stage.

If you use an alcohol marker, use the fine point nib for the fine detail and the wider nib for colouring larger areas.

The flesh parts covered by the chiffon straps are coloured to illustrate that the fabric is transparent. ▶

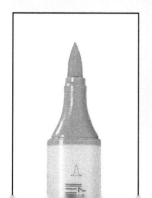

A second layer of colour is added on the opposite side of the light source to represent shadows.

Shading are added to the legs, arms, neck and face. You can use a second colour for this step.

Remember to add shading where one object casts shadows over another, such as underneath the chin, the nose and on the forehead, below the hair.

▶

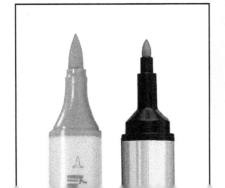

Chapter 5: The Fashion Illustration

You can do the shadows of the hair first, or do it as a final layer at the end. The hair around the face should be the darkest, due to the shadows of the face and the neck. You can shade the hair with a mid-tone colour, a darker tone or a warm grey. ▶

Chapter 5: The Fashion Illustration

The whole area of the hair is now rendered. Using the same colour, adding a second layer of over the first layer will darken the shadow areas. ▶

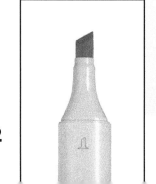

The inside of the dress is shaded first, because it will be the darkest and furthest from the viewer. This forms a basis for the depth that needs to be achieved. Folds such as these should be shaded like you would render cylindrical shapes.

The column-like folds shows that there is more volume than a simple A-line silhouette. In this drawing, the hemline demonstrates which folds curve towards the front and which folds curve towards the back. Always keep the basic shapes in mind when you draw fabric folds. ▶

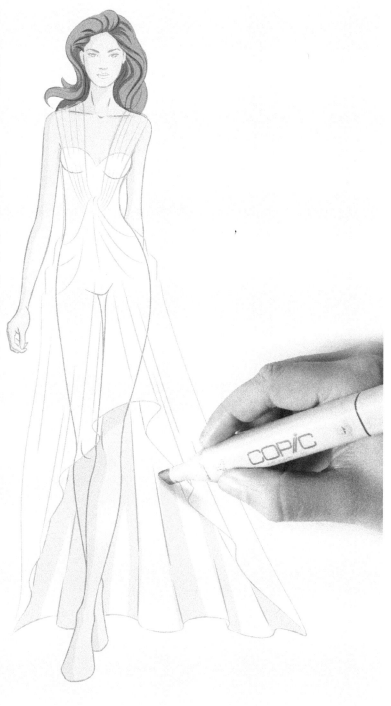

Chapter 5: The Fashion Illustration

The chiffon straps are now coloured using a thinner brush marker.

All the areas of the chiffon where shadows would fall are rendered. Areas that represent highlights are left open.

Reserving white areas demonstrate how the fabric shines. The inside of the folds at the front are coloured with a darker colour. ▶

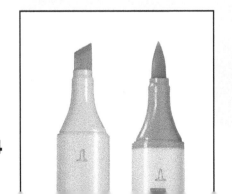

Chapter 5: The Fashion Illustration

Layering with transparent mediums, such as alcohol marker or watercolours, will create darker tones to represent darker shadows. A layer of colour is added to the left side of the dress as a whole. The shoes are coloured with a darker tone that ties in with the dress. ▼

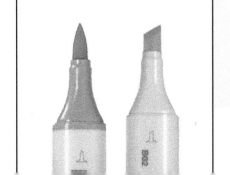

The face is coloured next. Colours that create unity with the hair and dress can be used for a sense of balance. The colours of the facial features should compliment the dress.

For the lips, a colour that stands out can create a focal point, but be careful to not over render this part as it will need subtlety. ▶

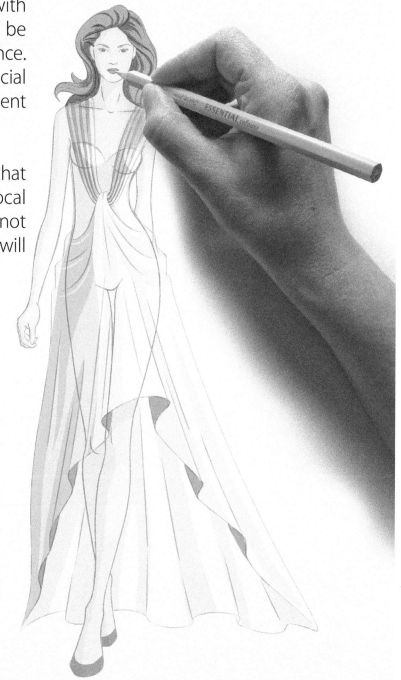

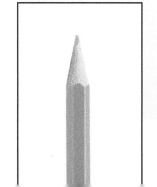

Chapter 5: The Fashion Illustration

The pencil lines are inked with a black fineliner. This is not necessary but it will add more definition to the illustration. You may also want to use a technical pen or dip pen for this step. ▶

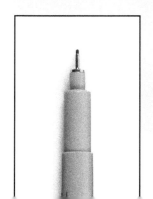

Chapter 5: The Fashion Illustration

Darker shadows are rendered on the inside of the dress, and underneath the chin. A transparent cool grey alcohol marker works well for generic shadows. Using it in more than one area will help to create cohesion and balance.

Highlights are added to the hair, body and the dress. Use a medium that is opaque such as a white pastel pencil, correction fluid or white acrylic paint. ▶

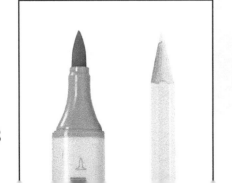

Chapter 5: The Fashion Illustration

Fashion Illustration Drawing Techniques © *Mila Markle*

Example 2

◀ The pose of the figure should compliment the chosen design.

Chapter 5: The Fashion Illustration

The garment consists of a short, slim fitting dress with a skirt over it. The skirt is made from a sheer fabric, which means that the dress will be visible underneath.

As a starting point for the rendering, some subtle shading is added to the hair and face using a grey alcohol marker.

When you are satisfied with the line drawing, you can start rendering. ▶

The flesh is rendered first as it will be covered with the dress and skirt for the most part.

Instead of colouring the entire flesh area, only those parts opposite to the light source are coloured. This creates a different effect. The parts of the hair that are darker are also rendered.

The parts of the legs covered by the chiffon skirt are rendered. Keep in mind that due to the transparency, the legs will still need to be visible at the end. ▶

Chapter 5: The Fashion Illustration

The top part of the dress is coloured here with a blue, medium tone colouring pencil in conjunction with a light blue alcohol marker.

Using a darker tone for shading will create definition.

Texture is created with the marker by making "speckles" over some parts of the colouring pencil. ▶

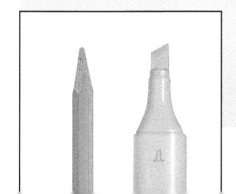

The whole dress is now coloured with the same light blue marker as well as pencil before proceeding to the sheer (transparent) garment.

Next, the shaded parts of the skirt is drawn by using a purple brush marker, overlapping the blue pencils and marker fills of the dress.
Keep your light source consistent.

The entire area of the hair is coloured and the shoes are rendered with a colour that matches the dress. ▶

◀ Some additional subtle colour is added to the face, especially for the lips and eyelids that need makeup.

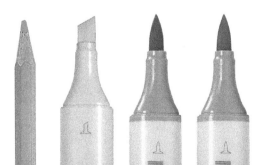

Chapter 5: The Fashion Illustration

The skirt is rendered further using a blush-pink colouring pencil. Paying attention to make those areas darker that will have more shade (such as the inside of the skirt and parts behind the legs). ▶

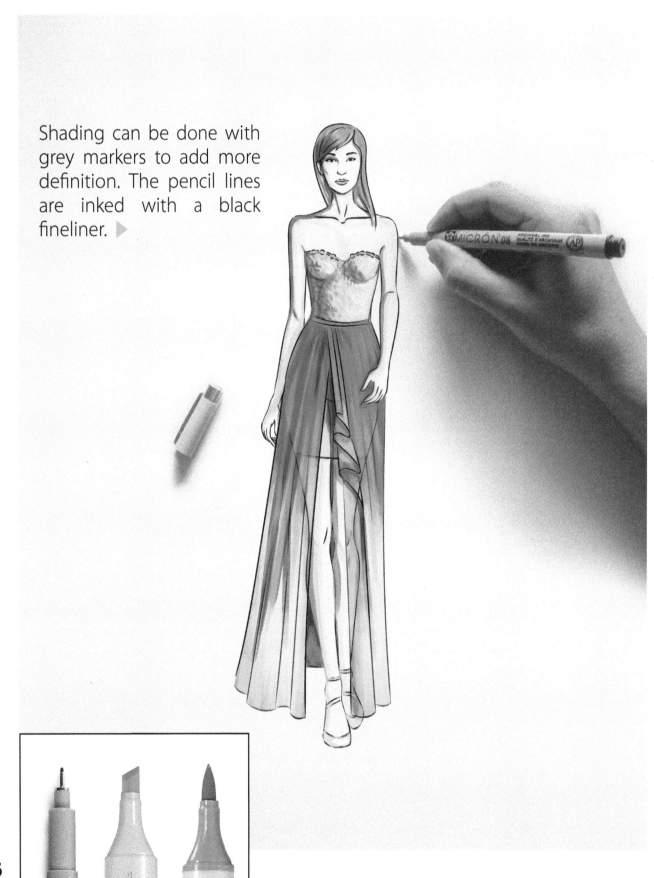

Shading can be done with grey markers to add more definition. The pencil lines are inked with a black fineliner. ▶

Chapter 5: The Fashion Illustration

Highlights are added to the hair, body and to the garment. The highlights and shadows in the top part of the dress creates texture. Highlights added to the folds of the skirt, shows the reflective nature of the fabric. ▶

Fashion Illustration Drawing Techniques © *Mila Marble*

Chapter 5: The Fashion Illustration

Create your own Illustrations

Rough Drawings

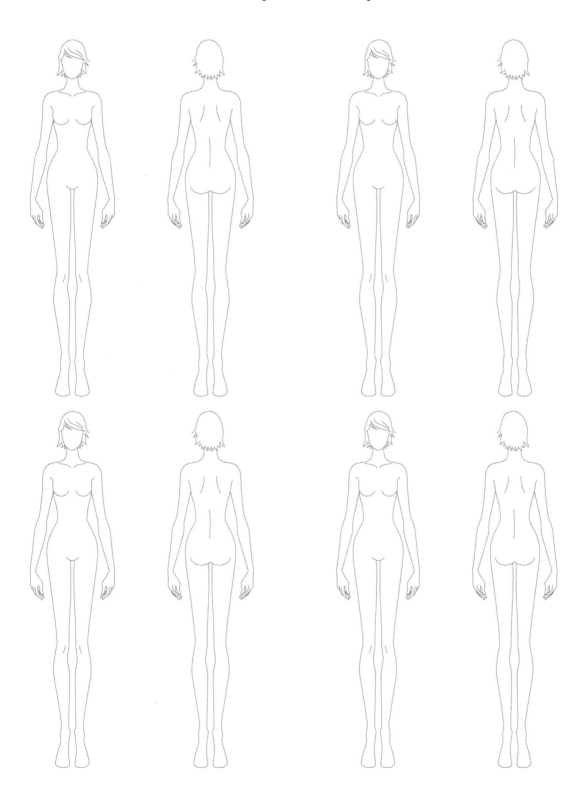

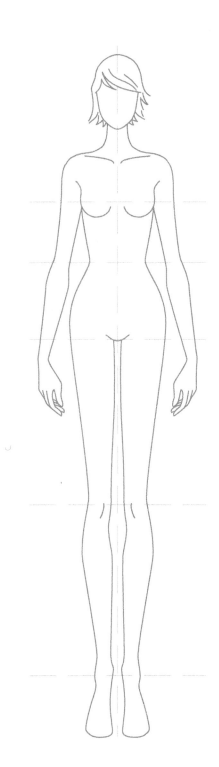
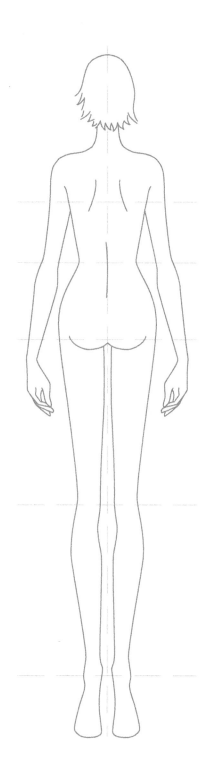

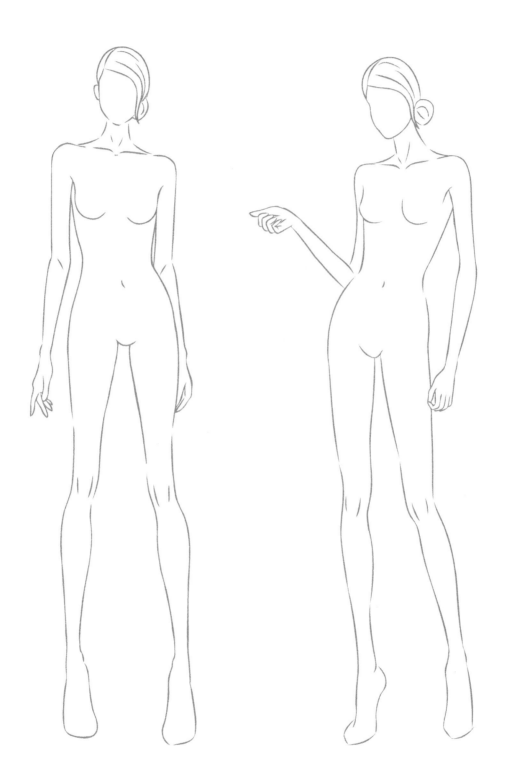

Fashion Illustration Drawing Techniques   © Mila Markle

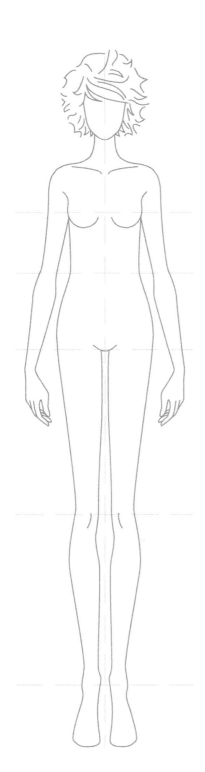
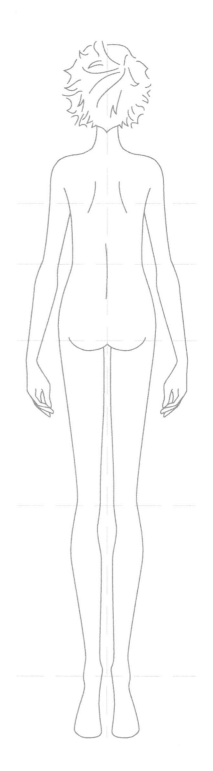

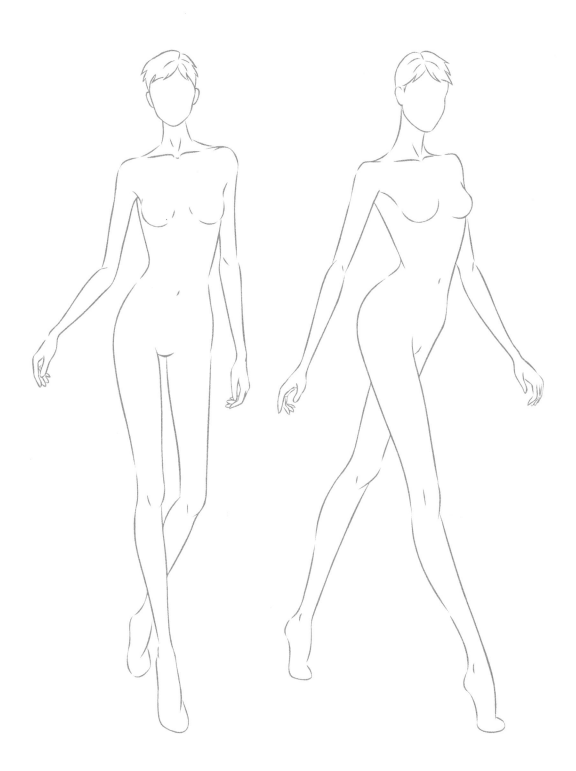

Technical Flat

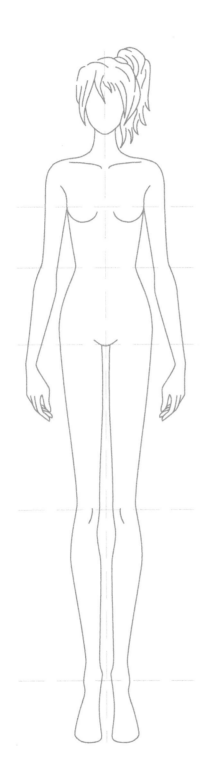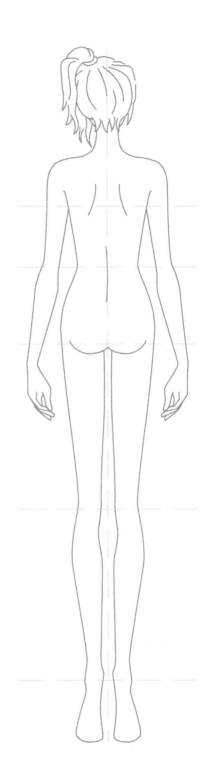

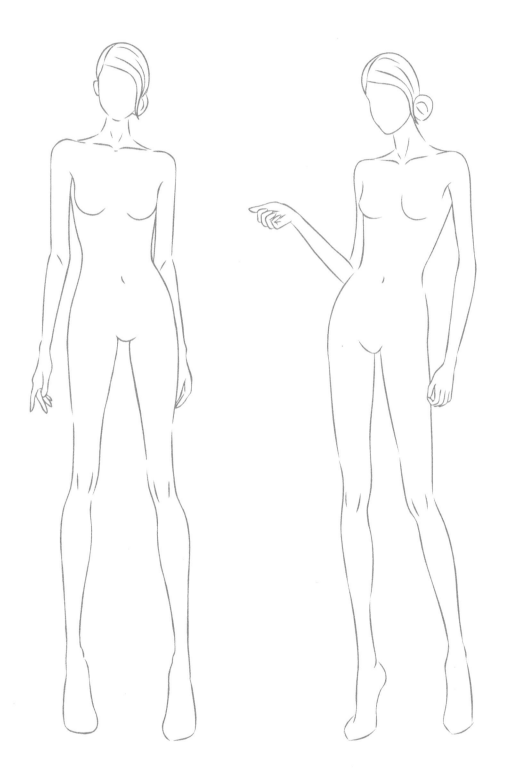

Technical Flat

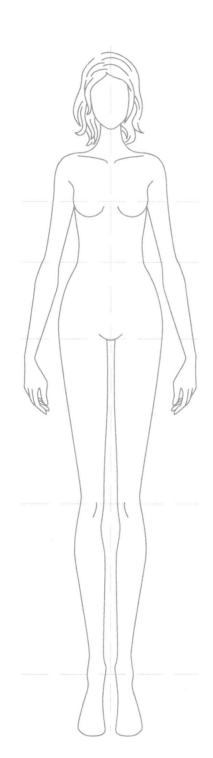
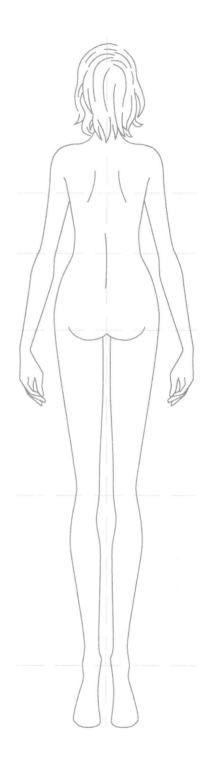

Fashion Illustration Drawing Techniques

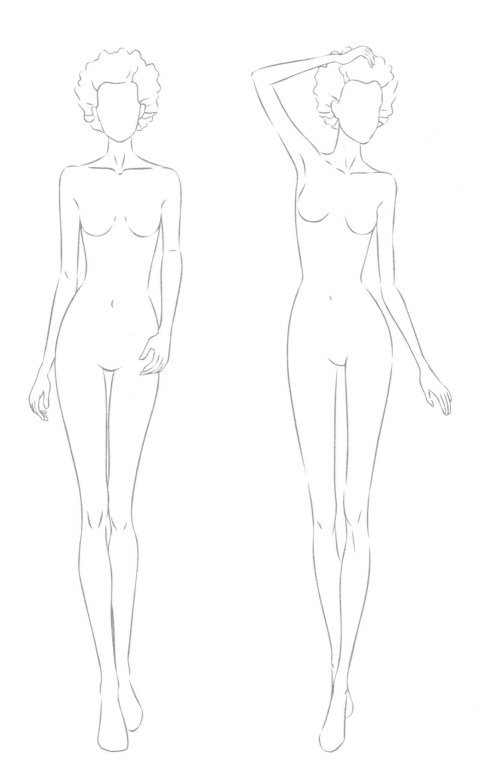

Technical Flat

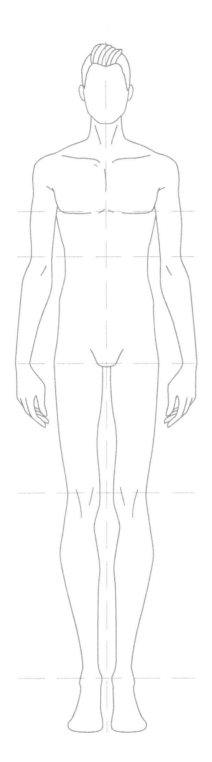
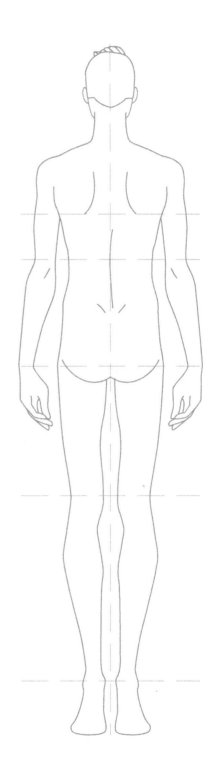

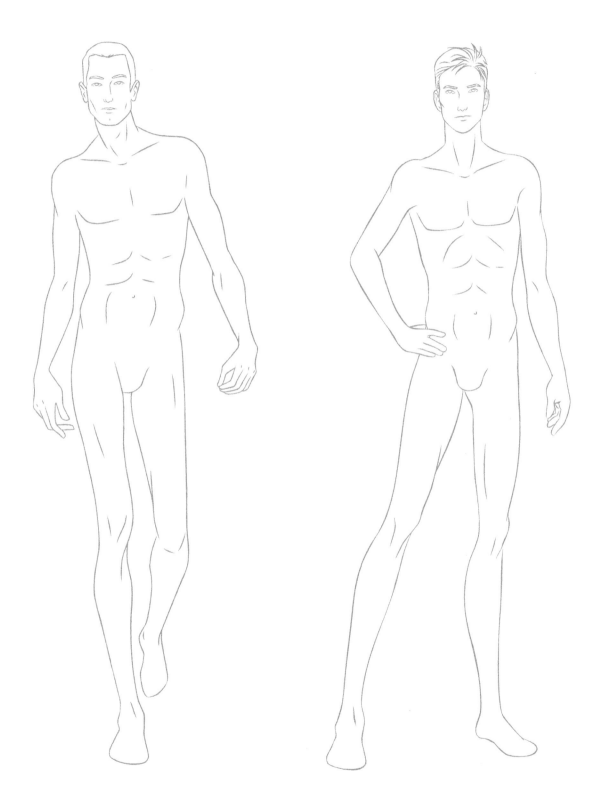

**Thank you for purchasing this book!
Book REVIEWS are greatly APPRECIATED!**

9 781776 449057